First Facts®

SCIENCE **BASICS**

WHAT IS MAGNETISM?

by Mark Weakland

Consultant:
Paul Ohmann
Associate Professor
College of Arts and Sciences: Physics
University of St. Thomas

PEBBLE
a capstone imprint

First Facts are published by Pebble,
1710 Roe Crest Drive, North Mankato, Minnesota 56003
www.mycapstone.com

Library of Congress Cataloging-in-Publication Data
Library of Congress Cataloging-in-Publication data is available on the Library of Congress website.
ISBN 978-1-9771-0272-0 (library binding)
ISBN 978-1-9771-0510-3 (paperback)
ISBN 978-1-9771-0276-8 (eBook PDF)

Editorial Credits
Jaclyn Jaycox and Mari Bolte, editors; Kyle Grentz, designer; Eric Gohl, media researcher; Laura Manthe, production specialist

Photo Credits
Alamy: Henry Westheim Photography, 15; Capstone Studio: Karon Dubke, 20–21; Shutterstock: Brian Goodman, 5, haryigit, 9 (top), J. Lekavicius, 17, Jakinnboaz, 11 (bottom), Nilobon Sweeney, 9 (bottom), Pixel 4 Images, 19, saicle, background (throughout), ShutterStockStudio, cover, 7, Valentyn Volkov, 11 (top), worradirek, 13

Printed in the United States 5960

TABLE OF CONTENTS

AN INVISIBLE FORCE

What can make things move but cannot be seen? It's not magic. It's ***magnetism***.

Magnetism is a force. It can pull and push on objects. But the force is invisible. Let's find out more about magnetism and how it works.

magnetism—the natural force of a magnet, which pulls it to iron or steel

PUSH AND PULL

Magnetism comes from electrical ***currents***. A current is the flow of electrical charges, such as ***electrons***, through an object. The movement of these charges makes a ***magnetic field***. A magnetic field around a magnet can create a force on objects in this area.

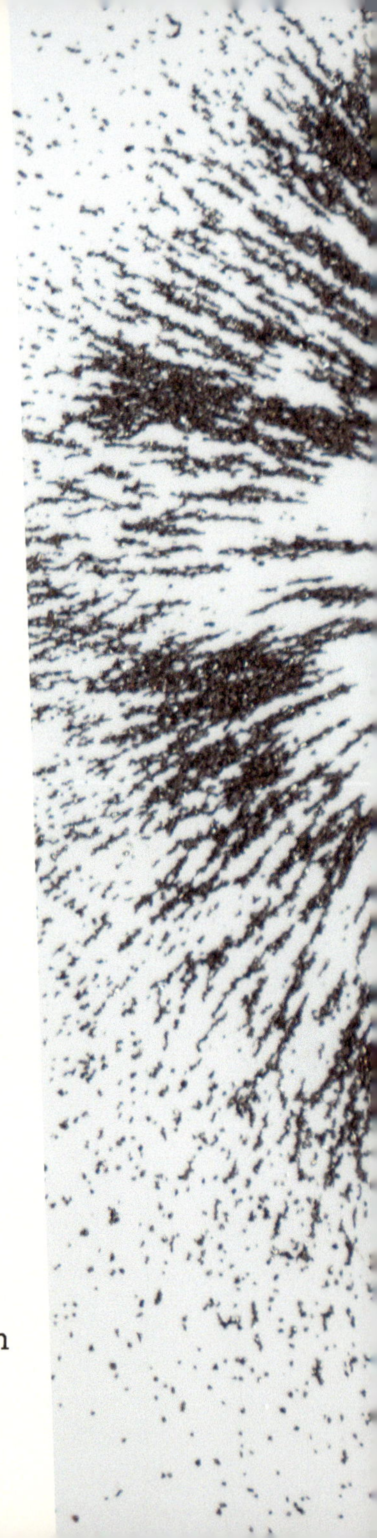

current—the movement of electrical charges in a certain direction

electron—one of the tiny particles that makes up an atom

magnetic field—an area around a magnet or electrical current that can produce a force on other objects

SEEING INVISIBILITY

Iron filings make it possible to see the outline of a magnetic field. Small pieces of iron scattered around a magnet line up in the invisible field.

KINDS OF MAGNETS

There are two basic kinds of magnets. A temporary magnet is made with electricity. This magnet can be turned on and off. A permanent magnet does not need electricity. Its magnetism is always working. A nail is an example of a temporary magnet. A refrigerator magnet is a permanent magnet.

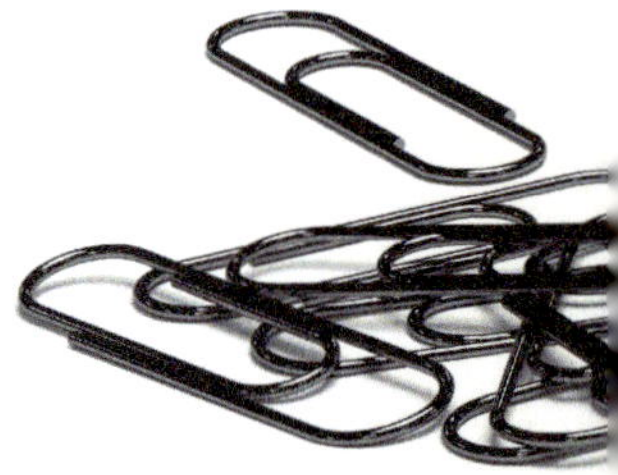

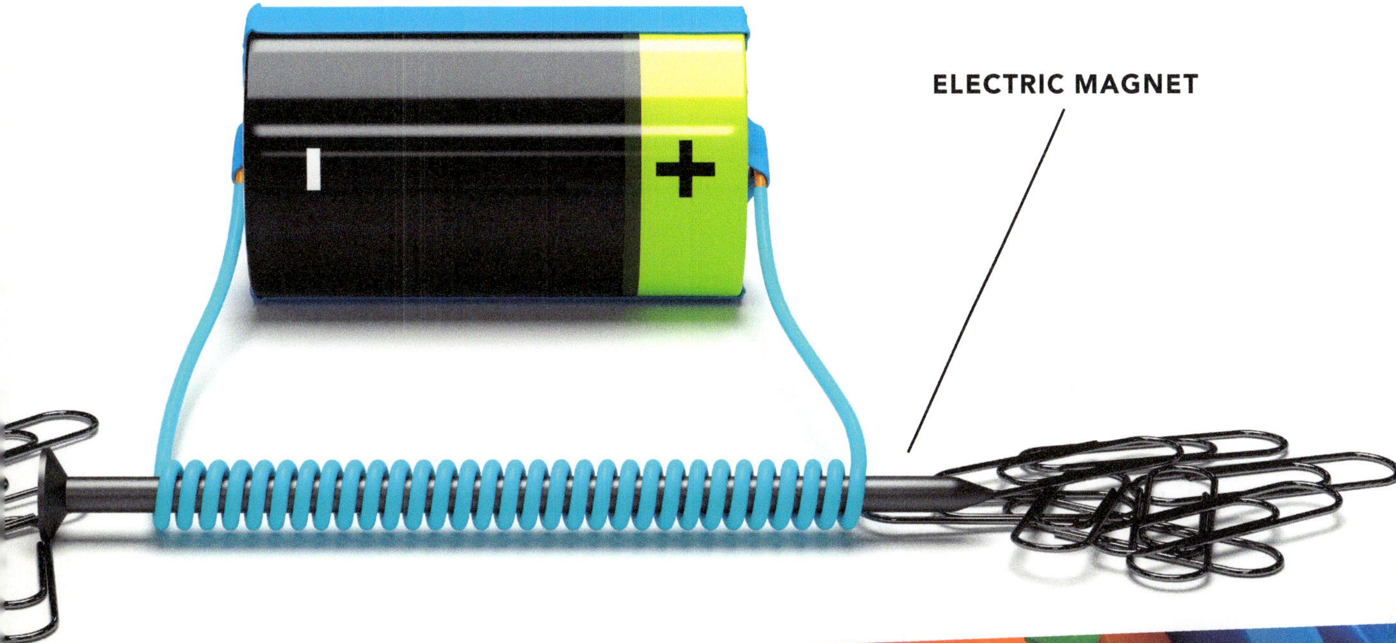
ELECTRIC MAGNET

MAGNETIC **POLES**

A magnet has two ends called ***poles***. These areas have the strongest magnetic field. There is a north pole and a south pole. Opposite poles pull together. Matching poles push away from each other. For example, a north and south pole will pull together. But two south poles will always push apart.

pole—one of the two ends of a magnet

NORTH AND SOUTH

More than 1,000 years ago, the first ***compass*** was made in China. It was a needle that acted as a magnet floating in a bowl of water. The needle always lined up in the north-south direction.

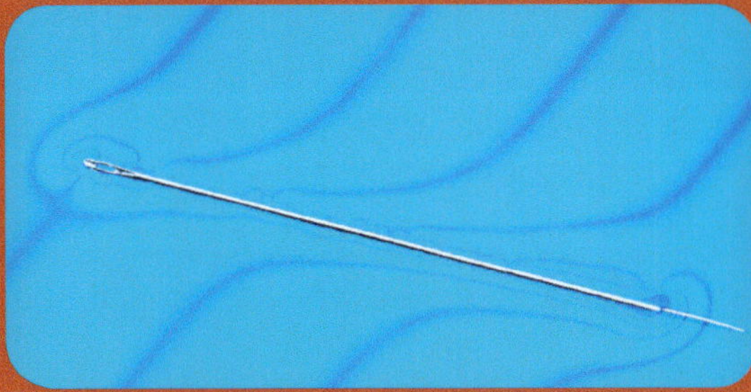

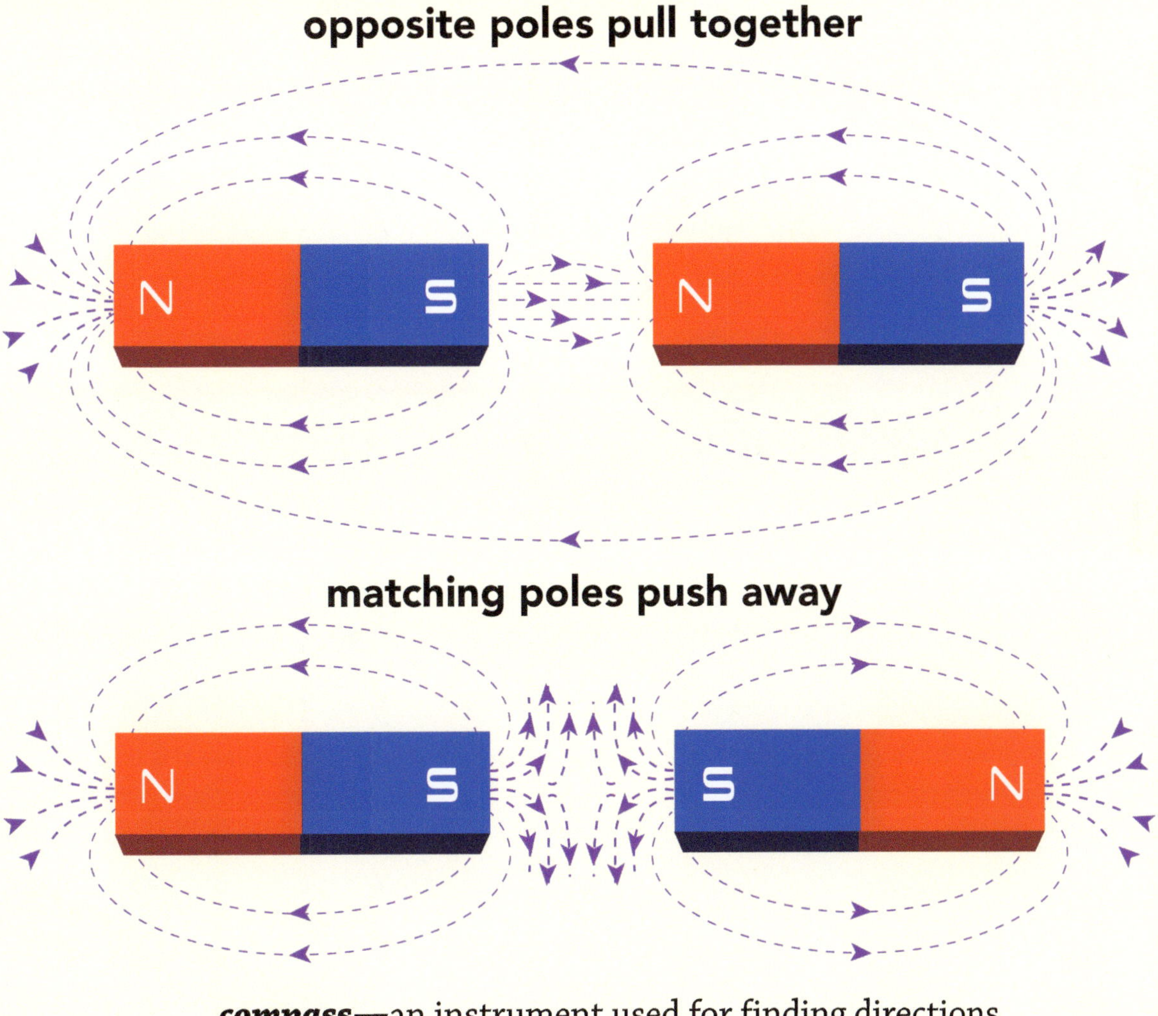

compass—an instrument used for finding directions

MAGNETIC **MATERIALS**

Some materials are attracted to magnets. Iron, nickel, cobalt, and most kinds of steel are common magnetic materials. This is why magnets stick to steel refrigerator doors. But they do not stick to wood or plastic doors.

FACT

One of the world's strongest magnets is in Florida. It is stronger than 4,000 ordinary magnets. Powerful magnets like this one are used to study medicine and computers.

RIDE A MAGLEV TRAIN

Maglev trains move very fast. They do this by using magnets. Two sets of magnets move the train. One set of magnets pushes the train up. When the train is "floating," another set of magnets moves the train forward.

FACT

A maglev train in Japan is the fastest in the world. The train whizzes by at 374 miles (602 kilometers) per hour.

Shanghai Transrapid
SMT

ELECTRIC **CARS**

The electric motor in an electric car uses magnetism. The motor has a set of magnets. The magnets push and pull on a loop connected to a shaft. The shaft turns the wheels of the car. This ***cycle*** repeats over and over, making the car move forward.

cycle—a set of events that happen over and over again

FACT

Electric cars are becoming more popular. In 2017, almost 200,000 electric cars were sold in the United States.

MAKING **NOISE**

Speakers use magnets to make sounds. Each speaker has two magnets. The first one uses electricity. The second one does not. The first magnet gets stronger when a lot of electricity flows through it. These magnets work together to make a cone in the speaker move back and forth. The movement creates sound waves that we can hear.

CAN YOU HEAR ME?

Speakers can be found in many places and in many things. Sound systems have big speakers. Cell phones have tiny ones. Stadiums and movie theaters have speakers. Where else can speakers be found?

MAGNETISM EXPERIMENT

WHAT DOES A MAGNET ATTRACT?

MATERIALS:

- bowl of small objects such as safety pins, marbles, erasers, paper clips, candy, and keys
- string
- large magnet

WHAT YOU DO:

1. Make a list of the objects in the bowl.
2. Make a prediction about what will happen when you lower the magnet into the bowl. What objects will cling to the magnet? What objects will not? Write, draw, or say your prediction.
3. Tie a string around the magnet. Then lower the magnet into the bowl and move it around. Observe what happens. What objects cling to the magnet?
4. Check your prediction. How does what you observed compare to your prediction?

GLOSSARY

compass (KUHM-puhs)—an instrument for finding directions

current (KUHR-uhnt)—the movement of electrical charges in a certain direction

cycle (SY-kuhl)—a set of events that happen over and over again

electron (i-LEK-tron)—one of the tiny particles that make up an atom

magnetism (MAG-nuh-tis-uhm)—the natural force of a magnet, which pulls it to iron or steel

magnetic field (mag-NET-ic FEELD)—an area around a magnet or electrical current that can produce a force on other objects

pole (POHL)—one of the two ends of a magnet

READ MORE

Adler, David A. *Magnets Push, Magnets Pull.* New York: Holiday House, 2017.

James, Emily. *The Simple Science of Magnets.* Simply Science. North Mankato, Minn.: Capstone Press, 2018.

Roman, Nora. *Using Magnets.* Super Science Tools. New York: Gareth Stevens Publishing, 2018.

INTERNET SITES

Use FactHound find Internet sites related to this book.

1. Visit *www.facthound.com*
2. Just type in 9781977102720

CRITICAL THINKING QUESTIONS

1. How do people know that an invisible magnetic field surrounds a magnet? Use words and phrases from this book to form your answer.
2. The book discusses many uses for magnets. How would you use magnets?
3. What machine could you make from two bar magnets? What type of work would your machine do? Be sure to explain how the magnets make your machine work.
4. Use the internet to learn about the magnetic field that surrounds Earth. In what ways is Earth like a magnet?

INDEX